D. H. TURNER

Romanesque Illuminated Manuscripts in the British Museum

PUBLISHED BY
THE TRUSTEES OF THE BRITISH MUSEUM
1971

First published 1966
Reprinted 1971

SBN 7141 0449 3

PRINTED IN GREAT BRITAIN
AT THE UNIVERSITY PRESS, OXFORD
BY VIVIAN RIDLER
PRINTER TO THE UNIVERSITY

ACKNOWLEDGEMENT

The writer would like to record his gratitude to Professor P. Lasko of the University of East Anglia and Professor K. H. Usener of the University of Marburg, from discussion with whom of a number of points in the book he has profited much.

LIST OF ILLUSTRATIONS

Front Cover

Park Bible, Initial 'S'. Additional MS. 14789, f. 83v. 'Mosan school.'
A.D. 1148.

In Colour

I. Shaftesbury Psalter, the Virgin and Child. Lansdowne MS. 383,
f. 165v. England. *Circa* 1130–50.

II. Stavelot Bible, Christ in Majesty. Add. MS. 28107, f. 136. 'Mosan
school.' A.D. 1097.

III. Floreffe Bible, the Crucifixion. Add. MS. 17738, f. 187. 'Mosan
school.' *Circa* 1150–60.

IV. Arnstein Bible, Design at the beginning of St John's Gospel,
incorporating the words 'In principio', Christ, the Evangelist and his
symbol of an eagle. Harley MS. 2799, f. 185v. Middle Rhineland.
Circa 1175.

In Black and White

1. Henry of Blois' Psalter, the Tree of Jesse. Cotton MS. Nero C.
iv, f. 9. England. *Circa* 1140–60.

2. Sherborne Chartulary, St John the Evangelist. Add. MS. 46487,
f. 86v. England. After 1146.

3. Stavelot Bible, Initial 'P': Samson and Delilah. Add. MS. 28106,
f. 84. 'Mosan school.' A.D. 1097.

4. Park Bible, Design at the beginning of Genesis, incorporating the
monogram 'IN', Christ in Majesty and scenes from Genesis. Add.
MS. 14788, f. 6v. 'Mosan school.' A.D. 1148.

5. Floreffe Bible, Initial 'P'. Add. MS. 17738, f. 208v. 'Mosan school.'
Circa 1150–60.

6. Medical Treatises, a physician. Harley MS. 1585, f. 13. 'Mosan
School.' *Circa* 1175.

7. St Bavo Sacramentary, the Crucifixion. Add. MS. 16949, f. 58v.
Flanders. Late twelfth century.

4

8. Siegberg Lectionary, St Maurice. Harley MS. 2889, f. 66v. Lower Rhineland. Second quarter twelfth century.

9. Arnstein Bible, Initial 'F': the Almighty. Harley MS. 2798, f. 102v. Middle Rhineland. *Circa* 1175.

10. Worms Bible, Initial 'A': the prophet Daniel. Harley MS. 2803, f. 253. Middle Rhineland. *Circa* 1160.

11. Gospel-book, Pentecost. Egerton MS. 809, f. 35v. Swabia (?) *Circa* 1100.

12. Psalter of Henry the Lion, the Purification and Moses and Malachi. Lansdowne MS. 381 I, f. 8. Westphalia. After 1168.

13. Monte Cassino Exultet Roll, Christ and Mary Magdalen. Add. MS. 30337. Southern Italy. *Circa* 1075.

14. Monte Cassino Psalter, Initial 'D'. Add. MS. 18859, f. 24v. Southern Italy. First quarter twelfth century.

15. Montpellier Bible, Initial 'O': the prophet Habakkuk. Harley MS. 4772, f. 293v. Southern France. *Circa* 1125.

16. La Charité-sur-Loire Psalter, Initial 'L': two monsters, and Initial 'C': the Resurrection. Harley MS. 2895, f. 72. Central France. Late twelfth century.

At one time Romanesque was the name loosely given to all the art of Europe between the Classical and Gothic periods which was considered to be 'Romanized', or dependent on Roman, Classical examples. Nowadays it is a term applied *par excellence* to the art of the Latin part of Christendom, excluding Mozarabic Spain, in the second half of the eleventh century and the first three-quarters of the twelfth. If we want to assign arbitrary dates to the beginning and end of the Romanesque period—and a style knows, of course, no exact limits—1049 and 1180 are convenient. In the former year Bishop Bruno of Toul became Pope as Leo IX, in the latter Philip Augustus ascended the throne of France. The first event marks the real beginning of the reform of the Western Church which was to reach its culmination in the pontificate of Gregory VII from 1073 to 1085 and make the twelfth century in popular parlance the 'Age of Faith'; the second event marks the real beginning of the progress of France towards becoming a nation and a great power. The two dates chosen introduce us at once to two fundamental characteristics of Romanesque. It, the first international European style, was preponderantly ecclesiastical art, art in the service of the Church and patronized by churchmen. Also, it was art in the creation of which France did not play the centralizing, synthetizing role she did in the Gothic period. At the start of the Romanesque period at least she was less a single state than an alliance of feudal principalities, in which the king was weaker than many of his vassals. The country with the strongest central authority in Europe was England after the Norman Conquest, but large unitary states were unknown at the time.

We are not surprised to find, then, that Romanesque had no one centre. Its internationality was a true one, not the result of the dominance of the style of one region over others. Whereas previous revivals of civilization in the West had been essentially regional, even racial, and so had previous mediaeval styles, the 'Twelfth-Century Renaissance', which coincides with the Romanesque style, was the first to possess an international character. Nationalism as we know it now, with its restricting influences and jealousies, was not yet developed in the eleventh and twelfth centuries. The strongest force in Europe was the Church and her supra-national character informed that of the artists who worked for her. As might be expected, it is associated with the great cathedrals and monasteries that we find these craftsmen, especially the illuminators of manuscripts, for book learning was essentially a profession for the clergy. 'A cloister without a library is like a castle without an armoury'—so wrote Canon Godfrey of Sainte Barbe-en-Auge about 1170. We shall meet several of the ecclesiastical centres of book production in our survey of Romanesque illumination in the British Museum, but others, including some of the greatest, such as Salzburg and Cîteaux, unfortunately cannot be represented from the national collection. The reader should bear this in mind and supplement what he finds now from other sources, if he wants a complete picture of the varieties of style in our field of study.

The appearance of Romanesque in English illumination was not until after the Norman Conquest. Indeed, from 1066 till about 1120 real pictorial art was in abeyance in this country. The Albani Psalter,[1] executed probably at St Albans for Christina, an anchoress at Markyate, some time before 1123 and now belonging to the church of St Godehard at Hildesheim, is the first great monument of English Romanesque miniature painting. The sources of its style are not so much indigenous — Anglo-Saxon — as Continental — Ottonian and Byzantine. It is in the work of the Liuthar school of Ottonian illumination that we see the prototypes of the long, slender figures, with grave expressions, that look out at us from the pages of the Hildesheim manuscript. A later version of its style, and one that has become more acclimatized, occurs in the Shaftesbury Psalter, Lansdowne MS. 383.[2] This was apparently made about 1130–50 for a lady connected with Shaftesbury Abbey in Dorset, the largest nunnery in England. In its miniatures the longitudinal style of the Albani Psalter has become something rounder and more solid. Figures, like those of the Virgin and Child adored by the owner of the manuscript (f. 165v; Colour plate I), are distinctly statuesque and have real weight. Their rich draperies show elliptical curves and folds, which are, however, largely artificial in their arrangement. They are examples of a constant feature of Romanesque illumination, namely that it always tries to schematize form, a tendency which it learnt from Byzantine art of the tenth to eleventh centuries. By a similar convention figures like those in the Shaftesbury Psalter are posed and deliberate. Their gestures, and even their expressions, can be described as ritual ones. We might even go so far as to speak of 'liturgical' art.

The type of book of which the Lansdowne manuscript is one, a psalter, was the standard manual of devotion in our period. Many surviving Psalters can be described as 'private', in that they were apparently made for a particular person, whose wealth and tastes their decoration may naturally be expected to reflect. One of the greatest men in Church and State in twelfth-century England was Henry of Blois, brother of King Stephen, munificent benefactor of the abbey of Cluny, sometime papal legate, abbot of Glastonbury 1126, bishop of Winchester 1129, and holding both offices till his death in 1171. He was well known as a connoisseur and patron, who surprised the local populace when they saw him, a grave and reverend seigneur, buying up old statues in the market at Rome. It may well have been for him that the Psalter, Cotton MS. Nero C. iv,[3] was executed about 1140–60. We do not know the exact place of its production, but this was probably Winchester, and Hyde Abbey there rather than the Cathedral Monastery of St Swithun is perhaps the more likely. Two of the thirty-eight full-page miniatures in the book appear to be direct copies of Italo-Byzantine paintings, the remainder are some of this country's finest Romanesque illumination. They have lost a good deal of their colour, but this only allows us to appreciate all the better the superb use of line in them. The drawing is done with great firmness and vigour which impart a strong dramatic force to the subjects. The peculiar drapery folds and patterns, which can be termed manneristic, are a speciality of English Romanesque, and rarely appear on the Continent, except in north-east France. In Henry of Blois' Psalter the linear, abstract tendencies, which had been so prominent in England in Anglo Saxon and 'Insular' times, have come to the fore again. They bring with them the temptation to ornamentalism which had run riot in a manuscript like the Book of Kells, and a miniature like that of the Tree of Jesse in the Psalter (f. 9; Plate 1) is more of a decorative design incorporating human figures than a representational picture. Rather than with such, its parallels are with the elaborate initials with which Romanesque books abound. However, it is essentially large scale and broadly designed despite its detailed ornament.

In place of the rounded style of the Shaftesbury Psalter Henry of

Blois' Psalter gives us something curvilinear and angular, which represents the main version of Romanesque in English painting. We find it in the Bible[4] illuminated for the abbey of Bury St Edmunds probably about 1130–40 by a secular artist, Master Hugo; in the Bible now at Lambeth,[5] executed about 1150 probably at Canterbury; in the earlier work in the Winchester Bible,[6] which is about the same date as Henry of Blois' Psalter; and in the frescoes in St Anselm's chapel in Canterbury Cathedral. It is a great style and stands not only geographically at one of the poles of Romanesque. At the other extreme from the English linearism is the neo-Classicism of Salzburg. Other examples of our English style are the miniatures of the evangelists Mark and John (f. 86v; Plate 2) in the Sherborne Chartulary, Additional MS. 46487.[7] This is not a true chartulary in the sense of a collection of copies of deeds. Executed shortly after 1146, it was designed for the abbot of Sherborne in Dorset to contain liturgical and legal texts which he would need in the exercise of his office as superior of his community. Despite their date its pictures belong to an early stage of the style we are considering, being closer to the more restrained Bury Bible than to the more extravagant Psalter of Henry of Blois or the Lambeth Bible. The Sherborne St John is also worth note as the only instance from this country in the twelfth century of a miniature of a standing evangelist. Not only his posture, but also the firmness of his contours remind us of a statue, or of enamelling or metalwork.

Closely connected with these two last types of art is the illumination which flourished in and around the valley of the Meuse in our period. This region, largely conterminous with the medieval diocese of Liège, was one of the chief foyers of Romanesque. A Romance-speaking enclave within the German Empire, it had a distinguished cultural history, exemplified in the schools of Liège and centres of monastic reform like Stavelot. For ever associated with the names of the metalworkers Renier de Huy and Godefroid de Claire, the 'Mosan style' enjoyed considerable excellence and influence. Its first great work was the Stavelot Bible, Add. MSS. 28106 and 28107. A colophon in this tells us how its two volumes were written continuously but carefully during nearly four years, and both completed in every respect: 'writing, illumination and binding' in 1097, though the second volume was actually finished before the first. As workers on the manuscript, Goderannus and his helper Ernesto are named. The former had been a monk of the abbey of Lobbes, in Hainault, for which he had completed a Bible (now at Tournai) in 1084.[8] Subsequently he must have transferred to the abbey of Stavelot, on the eastern boundaries of Belgium, of which he became dean and where the 1097 Bible was presumably executed. At least four craftsmen were responsible for its decoration, one of whom, by no means the best, may be confidently identified as Goderannus. One of the illuminators was strongly influenced by contemporary Byzantine art and another seems to have drawn on Late Classical sources. This artist executed some very fine drawings, such as that in the initial 'P' for the beginning of the Book of Judges, which represents probably not the death of Sisera as has been thought, but Samson and Delilah (f. 84; Plate 3). The figures are only shaded, most delicately, and the colouring present in the illumination may be considered an addition by another hand. Indeed, a collaboration of artists seems to be traceable in several of the initials in the Bible. In spite of its subject the scene we illustrate is remarkably gracious and soft. The composition is expert, with the half-circle of the main group contrasted with the single upright of the Philistine to the left, and the whole rendering suggests a more than one-dimensional archetype.

There is only one full-page miniature in the Stavelot Bible (Add. MS. 28107, f. 136; Colour plate II) and it is one of the masterpieces of Romanesque art. Its representation of Christ in Majesty, with the symbols of the four evangelists, may stand as a Western counterpart to the contemporary mosaic of the Pantocrator at Daphni, near Athens. Each may be taken as typifying the attitude to its Master of that branch of the Church to which it belongs. The Christ of Daphni is terrifying and fanatic, the Christ of Stavelot awe-inspiring and dignified. Western and Eastern spirituality, as in the classic definition of Abbot Butler, seem to be perfectly expressed in the two portrayals. There is work earlier in the eleventh century at Stavelot which foreshadows the Christ of 1097 and its ultimate source is probably Ottonian illumination such as is found in the work of the artist known as the 'Master of the Registrum Gregorii', who was employed by Archbishop Egbert of Trier (977–993) and undoubtedly drew on Classical models. In his famous miniature of St Gregory the Great[9] we find the origins of the style of the Stavelot figure, with its powerful impact, its sweeping lines and tremendous sense of volume, as seen in the swelling ovals over the breasts and left lower leg. The 'Master of the Registrum' is distinguished from other Ottonian illuminators by his rendering of volume in form as opposed to their predominant technique of flat stratification. Byzantine influence is not apparent in the Stavelot Christ, neither that of the humanistic type of painting which developed at Constantinople under the Comneni Emperors, whose dynasty came to power in 1081, or the older, ascetic type which shows itself in the Daphni Pantocrator. It has been claimed that the miniature is an addition to the Bible, a suggestion which does not seem necessary. Stylistically it could well be in existence by 1097 and it accords with other illumination in the manuscript, such as the drawings, which are certainly original. The Stavelot Christ's great descendant is the sculpture on the font executed between 1107 and 1118 for St Mary's church at Liège and attributed to Renier de Huy. The plastic qualities and chevron drapery folds of the figures on the font have their obvious origin in the style of the Stavelot miniature.

Amongst the religious orders founded in the Romanesque period was that of the Premonstratensian Canons, who became famous for their missionary activities in northern Europe. At their monastery of the Park, near Louvain, was written in 1148 a Bible, Add. MSS. 14788–90, from which we reproduce the page at the beginning of the Book of Genesis (Add. MS. 14788, f. 6v; Plate 4). At the centre of a design based on the monogram 'IN', within a rectangular frame, Christ is enthroned. In medallions round the frame are scenes from Genesis, and the 'field' of the page is filled with foliage, amidst the coils of which, and indeed growing from it, men, beasts, birds and a monster can be discovered. The whole conception is a thoroughly Romanesque one, with its mixture of illustration and decoration, sacred and profane, animate and inanimate, natural and unnatural. The inherent danger, to the austerely religious mind at least, is that the eye will be drawn from profitable mediation on the sacred illustration to unprofitable exploration of the vagaries and novelties of the profane decoration. It was against this kind of temptation that St Bernard inveighed in a famous passage, and its existence led the

Cistercian General Chapter about 1150 to rule that 'letters should be of one colour, and not painted'. In style, as might be expected, the Park Bible belongs to the Mosan school, its figures being flatter and more formal than the Stavelot Christ or drawn figures. However, it is not Mosan illumination at its most typical; there is considerable extraneous influence in it, and a number of hands at work. Some of the initials show German, Rhenish characteristics, and North French influence is particularly prominent throughout the book. This can be seen in the white foliage, of a kind favoured in the region centring on the abbey of St Amand, which ornaments many of the initials, in the bossed frame of the Genesis initial and in colours deeper and warmer than are usual in mid-century Mosan work. The zoomorphic initials which occur in the Bible (one, Add. MS. 14789, f. 83v, is reproduced on the cover of the present publication) are rare in Mosan books and again bespeak French influence.

The Mosan style at its height is seen in the illumination of a Bible, Add. MSS. 17737, 17738,[10] executed apparently for the Premonstratensian Abbey of Floreffe. Textual as well as stylistic evidence points to a date about 1150–60. It belongs to a group of books, all obviously the products of one workshop, the two other chief members of which are a Gospel-book from the Premonstratensian abbey of Averbode, now at Liège,[11] and a Gospel-book of unknown provenance, now at Brussels.[12] The exact location of the workshop from which they came has not been discovered. Stavelot has been suggested, but without conclusive evidence. The miniatures in the Floreffe Bible have cold, clear colours and strong, sharp outlines, which relate them at once to enamelling. There is pronounced schematization and hardness of form. In place of the sway and rhythm of the English illumination which we grouped round the Psalter of Henry of Blois we have something more abrupt and strained—with arms pressed close to sides by tight folds of drapery or shot out rigid in ecstatic gestures. The style is highly expressionistic in a ritualized, formalized way and probably influenced by the hieratic, ascetic tone which appeared in Byzantine art of the tenth to eleventh century.

In keeping with this bent is the introduction of allegory and typology into the miniatures. The Middle Ages had always had a weakness for this kind of exegesis, and nowhere did it influence Romanesque book-illustration so much as in the Mosan school and its dependencies. Thus, our illustration of the miniature at the beginning of St Luke's gospel in the Floreffe Bible (Add. MS. 17738, f. 187; Colour plate III) shows a representation in two compartments. Above is the Crucifixion, commented on by St Paul and King David. Beneath is the sacrifice of a calf, which is also St Luke's symbol, typifying the sacrifice of Christ. On either side are Luke, holding his symbol in its winged form, and King David, both uttering suitable comments. The whole idea derives from the fact that the calf is not only the symbol of the second evangelist but a traditional sacrificial victim. Similar compositions decorate the beginning of the other three gospels and at the start of the second volume of the Bible two full-page miniatures face each other. On the right are the Transfiguration and the Last Supper, on the left a presentation of the Active and Contemplative Lives, centring on the Seven Gifts of the Holy Ghost and the Three Theological Virtues: Faith, Hope and Charity. In relation to the Averbode and Brussels Gospel-books the Floreffe miniatures show an earlier version of the Mosan style. The other two manuscripts are more stereotyped and manneristic. Indeed, in them the abstract tendencies which were always strong in Romanesque have developed into anti-naturalistic ones, as they did in such an English manuscript as the Lambeth Bible. There are a few initials in full colour in the Floreffe Bible, but the majority are in black and brown outline, ornamented with foliage in red outline. Animate motifs are uncommon in them, the most usual, when it occurs, being a slender dragon, as in the 'P' at the beginning of the Acts of the Apostles (Add. MS. 17738, f. 208v; Plate 5). The outline Floreffe initials are of the highest quality and excellent examples of decorative design. Their symmetry is of another order to the exuberance of the initials in the Park Bible, and again recalls decoration on metal. Rather than with northern France, they have contacts with the Rhineland and Westphalia.

Mosan Romanesque had a glorious coda in the art of Nicolas of Verdun. In 1181 he completed the famous ambo at Klosterneuburg (the remains of which now form a retable) and in 1205 the shrine of the Virgin at Tournai. His hand has also been seen in the shrine of the Three Kings at Cologne and that of St Anno at Siegburg. Most of his work belongs to the Transitional style rather than to the Romanesque,

and its descendant is that great 'first Gothic' manuscript, the Inge-
burg Psalter in the Musée Condé at Chantilly.[13] Romanesque features
are strongest in the Klosterneuburg ambo and Nicolas's origins are
undoubtedly to be found in the Mosan style. We can see the kind of
thing which was his antecedent in two drawings of physicians in
Harley MS. 1585. This is a collection of medical tracts, without date
or provenance other than those suggested by its script and illustration. These imply the third quarter of the twelfth century and the
Mosan area. The illustrations comprise others besides the two we
have selected for special mention, including diagrams of how to per-
form operations, but these two stand out from the rest by reason of
their high quality. Plate 6 reproduces one of them (f. 13). The two
physicians are softer and more gracious than the figures in the
Floreffe Bible, but not so soft and gracious as the figures on the
Klosterneuburg ambo. Their drapery is more naturalistic than that in
the Bible and avoids the mannerism of the drapery in the Averbode
and Brussels Gospels. Its descent from the drapery style of the Liège
font and ultimately the Stavelot Christ can be clearly seen. Nicolas's
own drapery style was to develop into mannerism but its origins are in
the technique of the Harley physicians rather than that of the Floreffe
group of manuscripts. The closest resemblance between the former
and Nicolas's work is in the faces and hair. Here the approximation is
such as to incline us to bring the physicians near indeed to Nicolas
in time, to perhaps about 1175. One thing seems most likely, namely
that the workshop where they were executed, wherever it actually
was, was that where Nicolas was trained.

The Harley manuscript is the first completely secular book we
have discussed and is remarkable for this fact as well. The other
manuscripts we have treated have all borne witness to the preponderantly ecclesiastical character of Romanesque art, to which we referred
at the beginning of this study. Also, except for the Sherborne
Chartulary, which indeed includes several gospel lessons, their con-
tents have been in the main scriptural. Art in the service of
the Church was not, however, only required to decorate Biblical
manuscripts, whether the complete Bible or parts of it such as
Psalters or Lectionaries. Other books were needed for study, for
private prayer, and for the fulfilment of the Church's duty and

service of official prayer, known as the liturgy. These, too, received appropriate ornamentation. One of the most important of these other types of book was the Sacramentary, which contained the prayers used by the celebrant at mass. An example of an illuminated Sacramentary from our period is Add. MS. 16949,[14] excuted at the abbey of St Bavo at Ghent in the later twelfth century. As is traditional in Sacramentaries, and in the later Missals, the beginning of the prayer of consecration is marked by a representation of the Crucifixion (f. 58v; Plate 7). The tradition of such a representation arose from the likeness of the initial letter 'T' of the consecration prayer, or canon of the mass, to a tau cross. At first the initial itself was converted into a crucifix, the earliest example being in the Sacramentary of Gellone[15] of the end of the eighth century, but in time the representation of the Crucifixion became a separate illustration and the 'T' remained as possible of further decoration. This might take the form of a portrayal of Christ in Majesty or the celebrant at mass. Thus, the St Bavo Sacramentary gives us a separate miniature of the Crucifixion and at the start of the actual text of the canon Christ in Majesty. The figural style in the book is less manneristic than the kind of work we have been examining from the Mosan region, to which Ghent does not belong. The St Bavo style is much flatter than Mosan illumination, less 'worked up'. This enables us to notice at once the elongated shapes of the figures. Similar shapes were basic to the Floreffe style and, like the figures in the English Albani style, were an inheritance from Ottonian art.

The influence of the 'Mosan school' was particularly strong in the Lower and Middle Rhineland. In the former Cologne was the leading centre for manuscript illumination and as an example of its output may be taken the Lectionary, Harley MS. 2889, written in the second quarter of the twelfth century for the Benedictine monastery of Siegburg, some fifteen miles to the south-east of Cologne. In fact, it may well have been at Siegburg itself that the book was produced. It belongs to an interesting group of manuscripts, one[16] of which comes from the abbey of Gladbach, north-west of Cologne, and another[17] from the more distant St Emmeram's, Regensburg. This last may have been another product of Siegburg, which had close connexions with Regensburg, to which it gave its abbot as bishop in 1126. The

I. Shaftesbury Psalter, the Virgin and Child.
England. *Circa* 1130–50

II. Stavelot Bible, Christ in Majesty. 'Mosan school.' A.D. 1097

Siegburg Lectionary was for a long time thought to come from the monastery of St Pantaleon, Cologne, but has recently been restored to its true home. It contains miniatures both in full colour and shaded drawing on coloured backgrounds. Amongst them is a Tree of Jesse, in which the Tree is made to symbolize both the Tree of Life and the Tree of the Cross, and Jesse the First Adam over whose grave the second Adam was crucified. Of the two types of miniature in the Lectionary the drawn ones, such as that of Siegburg's patron St Maurice (f. 66v; Plate 8), are the more satisfactory. However, both types are of the same style, which has clear relations with definite Cologne illumination and with Mosan work. The Cologne-Siegburg style is broader and smoother than the Mosan one, as typified in the Floreffe Bible and its near relatives, and more inclined to monumentality. Both share, though, a similar treatment of drapery by 'built-up' oval and chevron patterns. A widespread technique in Romanesque times, this has been named the 'multiple-line' style. Of ultimate Byzantine origin, it was indeed the foundation of the English drapery style of the Henry of Blois Psalter. In England, however, it was adapted into a specialized version which has to be considered as a style on its own, as we have already inferred. The true multiple-line style appears at its most typical on sculpture of the second decade of the twelfth century at Vézelay, the Cluniac church where St Bernard preached the second Crusade in 1146, and both the Cluniac and Cistercian Orders probably played a large part in propagating the technique.

Closer to the mid-century Mosan style than the Siegburg Lectionary is such Middle Rhenish illumination as that in a Bible, Harley MSS. 2798 and 2799.[18] Together with a three-volume Passionary, Harley MSS. 2800–2802, and a copy of Rabanus Maurus's *De Laudibus Sanctae Crucis*, Harley MS. 3045, it comes from the Premonstratensian abbey of Arnstein, near Coblenz, where all three books may be presumed to have been written and illuminated in the period around 1175. The majority of the Bible's initials are in outline, mainly red. They are obviously inspired by Mosan initials and the Floreffe Bible was apparently a direct source, as one of the Arnstein initials seems to be an actual copy of the corresponding one in the earlier manuscript. The decorative foliage of the Arnstein initials is more organic than that in the Floreffe Bible. Especially in the first volume it terminates in large, exotic clusters of leaves. In the second volume it becomes flatter and looser. One of the initials, an 'F' at the beginning of the First Book of Kings (Harley MS. 2798, f. 102v; Plate 9) contains a fine standing figure, presumably the Almighty, in coloured outline. It has more delicacy than the Siegburg St Maurice and its slenderness brings it nearer to the Floreffe style than the Cologne one, which prefers a fuller representation of the human figure. It is more graceful than the Floreffe figures, but compared with the Harley physicians it is less advanced and less humanized—assuming that we may be allowed to keep the term 'gracious' for the latter, and apply the term 'graceful' to the present case, a subtle distinction certainly, but what is art criticism other than the making of such? The Arnstein figure is pure drawing, and we do not immediately think of some other technique, such as metalwork, when we look at it.

The four Gospels in the Arnstein Bible are preceded by elaborate compositions consisting of combinations of the opening words of the texts with representations of the evangelists. Thus, at the beginning of John (f. 185v; Colour plate IV) is a design in which the letters 'IN' have become little more than a trellis for a display of foliage. Down the right-hand side of the composition is the word 'PRINCIPIO', the letters of which are not immediately recognizable as such rather than as pieces of ornament. St John plays a somewhat minor part in the whole, appearing towards the top of the miniature, with his symbol, an eagle, and above him a half-figure of Christ. This full-colour Arnstein illumination is richer and stronger in tone than Mosan work. Colours are bright and burnished in contrast to the sombre, matt ones of the Stavelot Christ or the Floreffe miniatures. Paint is laid on more evenly, so that contours and outlines are less noticeable, or rendered by bands of colour. This is purely painting and does not remind us of some other technique, any more than the drawing in the manuscript did. Like the decoration of the outline initials in the Floreffe Bible, that of the Gospel initials in the Arnstein Bible is very balanced and organized. By comparison with the decoration of the Genesis monogram in the Park Bible it appears planned and professional. In general there is an expertise about the illumination of the Arnstein Bible which is in danger of becoming stereotyped.

A more original variety of Middle Rhenish illumination appears in a Bible, Harley MSS. 2803 and 2804,[19] which belonged to the church of St Mary at Worms in the late seventeenth century. The work in it is highly sophisticated, powerful and intense in spirit, with bright, clear colouring. Sculpturesque rather than metallic seems the epithet applicable to its figures, and several of the representations of the prophets (that of Daniel on f. 253 of Harley MS. 2803 is reproduced in Plate 10) are particularly striking. The style of the Daniel and some of the other prophets is so advanced that the proposed date of 1148 for the manuscript seems impossible, and one about 1160 must be preferred. The illumination of the Bible represents a combination of Byzantine and Mosan influences, with some subsidiary ingredients. The Byzantine influence is very noticeable in the faces of figures in the Bible and the Mosan influence in the decoration of initials. Some of these have close resemblances to initials in the Park Bible. Before the Worms style, however, it seems necessary to postulate the state of development reached by the Mosan style in the Floreffe Bible. There are also relations between the Worms Bible and the more northerly, and later, Arnstein Bible, for which both the figures and the decorative elements in the former may be cited. There are some drawn figures in the Worms Bible, but these look towards Swabian work rather than towards the 'Mosan school'. An extraordinary effect is given to the Worms painted figures by the contrast between their hard, clear outlines and their soft, rich surfaces. Peculiar are the gentle, elliptical folds on some of the draperies, which are quite unlike the folds found in Mosan or Byzantine illumination and to which it is difficult to find a parallel. The illumination that we see in the Worms Bible is quite distinct from the Lower Rhenish illumination which centred on Cologne and though both have their affiliations to the 'Mosan school', the lines of descent are separate and the results different.

Continuing our journey southwards into Germany we come to Swabia. One of the chief ateliers of illumination here was the abbey of Hirsau, which under the rule of Abbot William (1069–91), a former monk of St Emmeram's, Regensburg, became a great centre of religious life, where the customs of Cluny were introduced and from which many German houses were reformed. It has been tentatively suggested that a Gospel-lectionary, Egerton MS. 809, of about the year 1100 was executed at Hirsau. The manuscript has also been associated with the monastery of St Maximin, Trier, but without real evidence or much likelihood. Wherever it was produced, its illumination depends on that of the so-called 'Bavarian monastery school', which flourished in the monasteries of Tegernsee, Niederaltaich and Freising in the eleventh century. Compared with the great schools of Ottonian painting, this was rather a provincial one, but it is an important link between Ottonian and Romanesque. It kept itself remarkably free from Byzantine influence, developing a kind of 'anti-humanistic' spirit, of which we can find traces in the miniatures in the Egerton Lectionary. Despite their superficial brilliance and richness, they tend to rigidity and lifelessness. The compositions are completely two dimensional, with modelling and volume given a diagrammatic rendering. The impression of a picture like that of the Coming of the Holy Ghost at Pentecost (f. 35v; Plate 11) is of something pressed as flat as possible, and even splaying out in the process. This is an early state of Romanesque schematization of form. Subsequently it will be handled more skilfully and artists will learn, even if their picture has no recession, to try to give it a certain repoussé effect. At the moment however, the technique in the Egerton miniatures merely gives an idea of gaucherie, which is indeed a general characteristic of theirs.

The accession of Wibald of Stavelot to the abbacy of Corvey in Westphalia in 1147 brought that region into direct contact with the Mosan one. A comparable figure to Henry of Blois, Wibald was both a distinguished ecclesiastical and political statesman and furtherer of the arts. As his career is probably less well known than Henry's to English readers, we may spend some time on it, for it is an excellent example of a great patron's life in our period. Born in 1097, Wibald studied at Liège and took the Benedictine habit at Waulsort in 1119. Master of the schools there, and later at Stavelot, he was elected abbot of the latter monastery in 1130. Seven years later we find him in command of the Emperor Lothar III's fleet at the capture of Salerno from King Roger of Sicily. Immediately afterwards he was made abbot of Monte Cassino itself. The Emperor's subsequent withdrawal and the recovery of power by King Roger made it necessary for Wibald to resign the rule of Monte Cassino. A faithful servant of the next Emperor, Conrad III, he was named one of the two guardians of the latter's young son Henry, during the Second Crusade. Employed in papal and imperial embassies, he was returning from his second mission to Constantinople, when he died in Asia Minor in 1158. His body was taken back to Stavelot for burial. As evidence of Wibald's artistic interests we may cite the silver-gilt retable with scenes from the life of St Remaclus, the founder of Stavelot, and the head-reliquary of St Alexander which he commissioned for his Mosan abbey. The goldsmith Godefroid de Claire was his protégé. From Constantinople he brought back rich gifts and the Eastern Emperor Manuel I Comnenus joined with him in the cost of a gold retable to be ornamented with scenes from the passion of Christ and likenesses of Manuel's Empress, Irene, and Wibald himself. It is the internationalism of Maecenases, like the abbot of Stavelot and Corvey, which must have been amongst the most potent causes of the internationalism of Romanesque art.

Corvey was a leading centre of manuscript illumination in Westphalia, but was surpassed in importance by another monastery there, that of Helmarshausen. This house was patronized by Henry the Lion, Duke of Saxony (died 1195), who married Matilda, daughter of King Henry II of England, in 1168. At his command the monk Heriman of Helmarshausen decorated about 1175 a Gospel-book (formerly belonging to the Duke of Cumberland at Gmunden, in Austria) as a gift for the cathedral of Brunswick. To the same artist may be attributed a fragment of a Psalter, Lansdowne MS. 381 I,[20] which contains representations of Henry and his wife in the miniature of the Crucifixion (f. 10v). The Psalter appears slightly earlier in style than the Gospels, but must, of course, be dated after the Duke's marriage, or at the time of it. The Helmarshausen illumination has been related both to the Mosan style as found in the Floreffe Bible and its congeners and the style of the Siegburg Lectionary. The figures in the miniatures in the Gospels and Psalter of Henry the Lion are sharper and flatter than the Siegburg figures, and thereby closer to Floreffe. They have a hieratic character which straightway links them with Mosan art. The monumentality which we found at Siegburg and Cologne is missing and we are dealing once more with illumination that resembles enamelling. The patterned backgrounds which occur in the miniatures also relate them to metalwork, or to textiles. The effect aimed at in Henry's manuscripts is one of splendour in the tradition of Ottonian—and Byzantine—imperial art. We even find gold writing on a purple ground. Inevitably with reference to Helmarshausen we think of the goldsmith Roger, also a monk there, who flourished around 1100 and whose style comes out of the Mosan one. He was a pioneer of the multiple-line technique and of oblong panelling on drapery. The former occurs in our Gospel-book and Psalter, which also employ curvilinear shapes on drapery. Not infrequent too are cobweb-like patterns of lines on the garments. Both these last features relate Helmarshausen to England, in particular to the style of the Albani Psalter. In fact, Henry's connexions with this country were very close. He was a constant visitor to the Plantagenet court, at which he twice found refuge as an exile, and there are some striking resemblances to English art on metalwork executed for him. Like Mosan ones the Helmarshausen miniatures link New Testament subjects with the foretelling of them in the Old Testament, as on f. 8 of Henry the Lion's Psalter (Plate 12), with its representation of the Purification in the upper half of the miniature and the figures of Moses and Malachi prophesying in the lower half.

Italy gave much to the lands beyond the Alps in the eleventh and twelfth centuries, but her contribution to Romanesque book decoration is not on a par with theirs. There are no great original schools of Italian illumination in our period. From Milan and Lombardy there is nothing outstanding to chronicle. Central Italy is particularly renowned for its 'Giant Bibles', which, important as they may have been iconographically, cannot vie with transalpine productions in quality. Stylistically central Italy is a meeting-ground for influences from the north and the east (Byzantium). The south rises to a higher level, but even so, the style of its illumination is essentially derivative. Its figural work depends on Byzantine art, and it is as an example of Byzantine influence, and a medium for the transmission of this that we take note of it now. It represents a Greek graft onto Latin stock.

A speciality amongst south Italian manuscripts was illustrated texts on rolls of the Paschal Prophecy, or 'Exultet', sung by the deacon at the Easter Vigil. Their illustrations were often placed the opposite way up to the text, the purpose of this device being that, as the Prophecy was sung, the manuscript could be unrolled over a lectern and hang down in view of the bystanders, with its illustrations in the right position to be seen by them. Alongside religious and liturgical scenes, such as the Crucifixion and the Resurrection, or the Fall of Man and the Passage of the Red Sea, a feature of the Rolls was a representation of bees and a beehive. This is explained by the fact that the Exultet is sung over the Paschal Candle and contains references to the provision of wax for it by the queen bee. Finest of surviving Exultet Rolls is Add. MS. 30337.[21] Its execution may be assigned to the abbey of Monte Cassino about 1075. This house was the natural centre of spiritual and intellectual life in southern Italy and at the time with which we are concerned was ruled by the most distinguished of all its abbots after the founder, St Benedict, himself. Desiderius was a Beneventan aristocrat who preferred the cloister to the world and became abbot of Monte Cassino in 1058. His benefactions to the monastery and his buildings and restorations there were outstanding, chief of them being the new abbey church, dedicated in 1071. For his works craftsmen were imported from Constantinople, antique materials brought from Rome and objects commissioned in Constantinople. New manuscripts and gorgeous bindings are also mentioned by Leo of Ostia, his protégé and biographer, and an acrostic verse written in his time tell us that 'from regions as numerous and varied as the hillsides covered with leaves by the north wind did he gather various books'. In 1086 Desiderius succeeded Gregory VII as Pope Victor III, remaining still superior of Monte Cassino till his death in the following year.

The illustrations of the Exultet Rolls were first drawn in light brown ink. Some were coloured immediately, others only later, and frequently they were only shaded or tinted. Several of the miniatures on the Museum Roll are faded or rubbed, but enough remains for us to appreciate their fine drawing and delicate tones. Their spirit is that of Classical expressionism. It can be well seen in the representation of the fleeing Israelites on the far side of the Red Sea or that of the Risen Christ and Mary Magdalen in the Garden (Plate 13). This is a much more personal, humanized rendering than we are accustomed to in true Romanesque. The trees and vegetation are certainly formal and heraldic, but the two figures have a life and motion which are not the results of the cumulative effect of their component features but come from their execution as a whole. There are schematizations in the work, but they do not destroy form. The movement in the picture is natural and easy, not overcharged and dramatic, as it was in such a manuscript as Henry of Blois' Psalter. A miniature such as the one we are discussing is important because it shows already during the first phase of Romanesque north of the Alps the genesis of the Gothic spirit in southern Europe. We have referred earlier to the humanistic trend in painting in Byzantine art in the latter years of the eleventh century. In fact, it is not to this that the pictures on the Exultet Roll look, but to the classicizing style of the Macedonian Renaissance of the ninth to tenth centuries after the lifting of the Icónoclastic ban in the Eastern Empire. The balance of form and schematization in the Roll is similar to that found in such a famous Byzantine manuscript as the Paris Psalter of the end of the ninth century rather than to the technique of contemporary Constantinopolitan painting. Our Cassinese figural style is generally lighter in touch than Byzantine work. A good deal of this may be due to the technique employed, but some of it is probably a deliberate Western characteristic. It is worth remarking that there is no great resemblance between the miniatures on the Exultet Roll and the frescoes thought to have been put up in the church of Sant' Angelo in Formis, near Capua, in the time of Desiderius, which are much more hieratic and stylized, and conventionally Romanesque.

In contrast to the freshness and clarity of the illustrations on the Exultet Roll its initials come as a surprise. Interlace and foliage as developed as any north of the Alps decorate them. Again the style is derivative. The interlace, and the animal motifs that go with it, can only come from pre-Carolingian times, from the Hiberno-Saxon art of the British Isles. As a centre of Insular influence in Italy we have the abbey of Bobbio in Piedmont, founded by the Irish missionary, St Columban, in 612. The foliage in the initials comes from Ottonian Germany and there are plenty of connexions to explain this. The two abbots of Monte Cassino preceding Desiderius were Germans and there still exists in the Vatican Library the Gospel-book[22] which the Emperor Henry II presented to the monastery. This was illuminated

III. Floreffe Bible, the Crucifixion. 'Mosan school.' *Circa* 1150–60

· erar uerbum·et uerbum erat apud dm·et deus
erat uerbu·Hoc erat in principio apud dm·Oia
ppsa facta sunt·et sine ipso factum est nichil·

lumine. Erat lux uera·que illuminat omne ho
mine ueniente in hunc mundu·In mundo erat et
mundo per ipsum factus est·et mundus eum non cognouit·

IV. Arnstein Bible, Design at the beginning of St John's Gospel, incorporating
the words 'In principio', Christ, the Evangelist and his symbol of an eagle.
Middle Rhineland. *Circa* 1175

in the Ottonian school of Regensburg and manuscripts survive, made under Desiderius, containing work which depends directly on that in the Imperial gift. The Monte Cassino initial style in the first quarter of the twelfth century is shown us by a Psalter, Add. MS. 18859 (there are no miniatures in the book). Germanic foliage appears mostly in the lesser initials, the major ones being ornamented predominantly with interlace and animal forms (f. 24v; Plate 14). The writing which appears on the page we illustrate is the characteristic 'Beneventan script' practised in southern Italy from the eighth to the thirteenth centuries. The Psalter's initials are completely artificial. The orginally inanimate interlace and the animate animal shapes are fast becoming indistinguishable from each other, and equally fantastic and unreal. We see a style, the origins of which are far in the past, developed to its furthest extent and losing its life in the process. The result is too freakish to be regarded as a true manifestation of Romanesque. We have spoken of transalpine and Byzantine influences in connexion with south Italian illumination, but there is perhaps a further relationship to which we may allude now. Southern Italy was close not only to the Byzantine world, but also to the Moslem one. Is there not something of the endless repetitiveness that we associate with Islamic ornament in the initials of the Monte Cassino Psalter?

Unlike England or Germany, France had no great native schools of book illustration in the tenth to eleventh centuries, upon which to draw in the formation of her Romanesque illumination. It is not to be wondered at therefore that this was strongly influenced in its inception by foreign examples. These came naturally enough from the lands near which the different regions of France lay, in the north from England and the Low Countries, in the east from Germany and in the south from the Mediterranean countries. There resulted three broad divisions of French Romanesque book illustration, of which the southern one was the least traditional and the most eccentric. Whereas in the north and east of France illumination may be considered predominantly representational, although preferring schematization to naturalism, in the south it cultivates abstraction. Here we find a preponderance of diagrammatic figures and a delight in purely decorative ornament that recall pre-Carolingian art. Occurring also are a violence and turbulence of movement in the scenes that seem distinctly southern rather than northern. Southern French illumination of about 1125 is to be found in the British Museum in a two-volume Bible, Harley MSS. 4772 and 4773, which was given to the Capuchins of Montpellier in 1622. The script and decoration of the manuscript are alike typically Provençal (except for the first two initials, which are more conventional and probably additional). Highly impressionistic Biblical scenes and figures appear in the initials, together with strange ornamental flora and fauna. The general effect is barbaric, even rustic in places, but arresting. It reminds us at once of the proximity of Spain and its Christianized barbarian art, known as Mozarabic, and a particularly Spanish detail is the narrow interlace with its sharp angles that appears in the illumination. Draperies billow into fantastic shapes, as in the case of the prophet Habakkuk (Harley MS. 4772, f. 293v; Plate 15). This figure with his swirling cloak is the perfect counterpart in book illustration of figures on the famous Romanesque façade at Saint-Gilles in Provence.

The illumination of the Montpellier Bible exhibits a degree of pure experiment and divorce from reality which is ultimately sterile. Art may seek to improve nature as well as to represent and interpret it, but it cannot replace it. If it tries to do so, it risks becoming incomprehensible, because it cuts itself off from the realm of sense perception where all knowledge begins. Periodically it must look unto the rock whence it is hewn, nature, and this is what it started to do at the end of the Romanesque period, when the possibilities of schematic representation were becoming exhausted. The result was the Transitional Style between Romanesque and Gothic. As an example of Romanesque turning towards naturalism with which to close this essay, we have chosen the illumination of a Psalter, Harley MS. 2895,[23] apparently executed at the Cluniac Priory of La Charité-sur-Loire in the late twelfth century. Subsequently, about 1200, it probably belonged to the Benedictine nunnery of the Holy Cross at Poitiers. Every psalm in the book originally began with an illuminated initial, but unfortunately several of them have been cut out at sometime. Our plate (no. 16) reproduces f. 72, which includes Psalm 116, the initial 'L' of which is formed of two monsters, and part of Psalm 117, the initial 'C' of which contains a representation of the Resurrection. La Charité lies at about the meeting-point of our three regions of French illumination and the decoration of the Psalter does not really belong to any of them. More painterly and naturalistic than traditional French Romanesque, it shows considerable Byzantine influence. This influence was everywhere increasing in Europe in the second half of the twelfth century, and was one of the main causes of the revitalization of art then. It was not the only cause, however. Some of the revitalization came from within, and we can see this in the La Charité Psalter. Whilst such features as the solid, well-rounded treatment of flesh and the rendering of faces in profile are particularly Byzantine, the soft, loose draperies are not. They are a purely Western naturalization of the more artificial technique usual in Romanesque. The combination of movements that we have just found points to the fact that the genesis of a new style in art lies always in the interaction of external influences and internal developments.

The Romanesque period was the golden age of book illustration in Europe. Never before nor after did it rank so high and independently as a form of art, enjoy such widespread cultivation and excellence and so respond to the spirit of the times. These saw the zenith of the temporal power of the Western Church and of its mission as an agent of culture and civilization. We have already remarked how books were the especial preserve of ecclesiastics and probably at no other time in the history of Europe have the habitual users of books been in such positions of influence and responsibility as in the eleventh and twelfth centuries and books been so vital to a dominant class. We must remember that to the Romanesque churchman books were not just material for academic study or aids to recreation, their first and foremost purpose was the tradition of the precepts by which he attempted to lead the Christian life and many of their texts were actively required in the living of it. Christianity is after all a religion of a book, the Bible, and the performance of the liturgy a vital part of this religion. Hence the embellishment of scriptural and liturgical books, and afterwards of others, was a natural phenomenon of an age in which the Christian religion, in the persons of its clergy, was in the ascendant. The ideal of these clergy was one of asceticism and spirituality, of self-denial and the renunciation of nature. Inevitably therefore they tended to direct the art which was particularly theirs, book illumination, away from naturalism, and in keeping with this trend was the official view of illumination that it must remain book illustration, secondary and subordinate to the text it was decorating. The Romanesque principles of schematization of form and stylization of expression are essentially those of ornamental work rather than free representation. Artists, however, are notoriously wayward and liable to take a higher view of the importance of their craft than do their patrons. It is the conflict between the strict ideas behind Romanesque illumination and the natural expansiveness of its executants that gives this art its peculiar flavour.

NOTES

[1] O. Pächt, C. R. Dodwell and F. Wormald, *The St Albans Psalter (Albani Psalter)*, 1960; E. G. Millar, *English Illuminated Manuscripts from the Xth to the XIIIth Century*, Paris and Brussels, 1926, pl. 34.

[2] British Museum, *Reproductions from Illuminated Manuscripts*, series ii, pl. ix; G. F. Warner, *Illuminated Manuscripts in the British Museum*, 1903, pl. 13; Millar, pls. 32, 33.

[3] *Reproductions*, series iii, pls. vii–ix; Warner, pl. 12; Millar, pl. 44.

[4] Corpus Christi College, Cambridge, MS. 2: Millar, pls. 37–40.

[5] Lambeth Palace Library, MS. 3: C. R. Dodwell, *The Great Lambeth Bible*, 1959; Millar, pl. 41.

[6] Winchester Cathedral Library: W. Oakeshott, *The Artists of the Winchester Bible*, 1945; Millar, pls. 45–47.

[7] *Reproductions*, series v, pl. v.

[8] Grand Séminaire, cod. 1.

[9] A. Goldschmidt, *German Illumination*, vol. ii, Florence and Paris, 1928, pl. 7.

[10] *Reproductions*, series iii, pl. x; Warner, pl. 15.

[11] University Library, MS. 363c: A. Grabar and C. Nordenfalk, *Romanesque Painting*, Lausanne, 1958, p. 165.

[12] Bibliothèque Royale, MS. 10527: L. M. J. Delaissé, *Miniatures médiévales*, Brussels, 1959, no. 8.

[13] MS. 1695: J. Porcher, *French Miniatures from Illuminated Manuscripts*, London, 1960, pl. xli. There is a set of photographs of the manuscript kept as Facsimile 277 in the Department of Manuscripts at the British Museum.

[14] *Reproductions*, series i, pl. xxxiv.

[15] Paris, Bibliothèque Nationale, MS. lat. 12048: E. H. Zimmerman, *Vorkarolingische Miniaturen*, Mappe II, Tafel 154a.

[16] Pierpont Morgan Library, New York, MS. 563 and München-Gladbach Münster Archiv, MS. 9: M. Harrsen, *Central European Manuscripts in the Pierpont Morgan Library*, New York, 1958, pls. 29, 84.

[17] Bayerische Staatsbibliothek, Munich, Clm. 14055: H. Schnitzler, *Rheinische Schatzkammer: Die Romanik*, Tafelband, Düsseldorf, 1959, Tafel 70.

[18] *Reproductions*, series iv, pl. xii; Warner, pl. 18.

[19] *Reproductions*, series iv, pl. xi; Warner, pl. 16.

[20] *Reproductions*, series i, pl. xl.

[21] J. P. Gilson, *An Exultet Roll illuminated in the XIth Century at the Abbey of Monte Cassino*, 1929.

[22] Cod. Ottobon. lat. 74: Goldschmidt, pl. 78.

[23] *Reproductions*, series i, pl. xix.

BIBLIOGRAPHY

M. Avery, *The Exultet Rolls of South Italy*, Princeton, 1936.

T. S. R. Boase, *English Art: 1100–1216*, The Oxford History of English Art, volume iii, 1953.

A. Boeckler, *Abendländische Miniaturen bis zum Ausgang der Romanischen Zeit*, Berlin and Leipzig, 1930.

—*Deutsche Buchmalerei Vorgotischer Zeit*, Königstein in Taunus, 1953.

Bibliothèque Nationale, Exhibition Catalogue: *Les Manuscrits à Peintures en France du VIIe au XIIe siècle*, Paris, 1954.

British Museum, *Reproductions from Illuminated Manuscripts*, series i–v, 1923–65.

British Museum, *Schools of Illumination*, parts i–iv, 1914–22.

S. Collon-Gevaert, J. Lejeune and J. Stiennon, *Art roman dans la Vallée de la Meuse aux XIe et XIIe Siècles*, Brussels, 1963.

A. Grabar and C. Nordenfalk, *Romanesque Painting*, Lausanne, 1958.

F. Jansen, *Die Helmarshausener Buchmalerei zur Zeit Heinrichs des Löwen*, Hildesheim, 1933.

P. Lauer, *Les Enluminures romanes de la Bibliothèque Nationale*, Paris, 1927.

E. G. Millar, *English Illuminated Manuscripts from the Xth to the XIIIth Century*, Paris and Brussels, 1926.

J. Porcher, *French Miniatures from Illuminated Manuscripts*, 1960.

M. Rickert, *Painting in Britain: the Middle Ages*, The Pelican History of Art, 1954.

M. Salmi, *Italian Miniatures*, 1957.

O. E. Saunders, *English Illumination*, Florence and Paris, 1928.

H. Swarzenski, *Monuments of Romanesque Art*, 1954.

G. F. Warner, *Illuminated Manuscripts in the British Museum*, 1903.

PLATE I. Henry of Blois' Psalter, the Tree of Jesse. England. *Circa* 1140–60.

·S̄ IOHA NNES·

IN PRINCIPIO ERAT VERBVO · ET VERBVM ERAT

PLATE 2. Sherborne Chartulary, St John the Evangelist. England. After 1146.

INCP̄ LIBER IVDCV̄ :

OST
mortem
iosue. consu
luerunt filu
isrt̄ dn̄m di
centes· quis
ascendet ante
nos contra
chananeum,
& erit dux belli :·
Dixitq: dn̄s· Judas
ascendet · Ecce tradidi
terram in manus eius·
Et ait iudas symeoni fratri
suo· Ascende mecum in sorte
mea· &pugna contra chanane
um. ut &ego pergam tecum in
sorte tua· Et abiit cum eo symeon·
Ascendirq: iudas. &tradidit dn̄s cha
naneum acpherezeum in manus eorum.
&percusserunt in bezech decem milia ui
rorum· Inueneruntq: adonibezec̄ in bezec̄,

.ı.

.ıı.

PLATE 3. Stavelot Bible, Initial 'P': Samson and Delilah. 'Mosan school.'
A.D. 1097.

PLATE 4. Park Bible, Design at the beginning of Genesis. 'Mosan school.'
A.D. 1148.

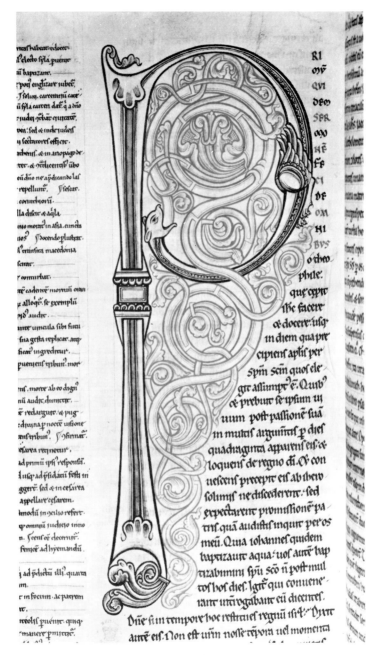

PLATE 5. Floreffe Bible, Initial 'P'. 'Mosan school.' *Circa* 1150–60.

PLATE 6. Medical Treatises, a physician. 'Mosan school.' *Circa* 1175

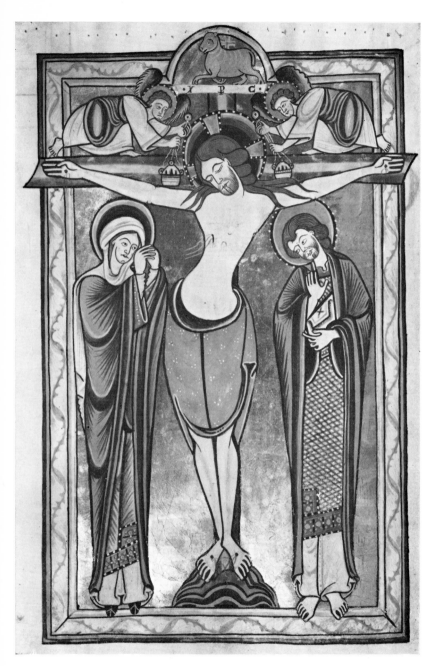

PLATE 7. St Bavo Sacramentary, the Crucifixion. Flanders. Late twelfth century.

PLATE 8. Siegburg Lectionary, St Maurice. Lower Rhineland. Second quarter twelfth century.

PLATE 9. Arnstein Bible, Initial 'F': the Almighty. Middle Rhineland.
Circa 1175.

CIPIT·LIBER·DAHI
ELIS·PPHETE··

NO · TER CIO
REGHI IOACHIH REGIS IVDA./ UEHIT
nabuchodonofor rex babilonif ierufa
lem./ etobfedit eam. Et tradidit dñf in
manuf eiuf ioachin regē iude. et par-
tem uafoz dom° dñi./ et afportauit ea in

PLATE 10. Worms Bible, Initial 'A': the prophet Daniel. Middle Rhineland.
Circa 1160.

PLATE II. Gospel-book, Pentecost. Swabia (?). *Circa* 1100.

PLATE 12. Psalter of Henry the Lion, the Purification and Moses and Malachi.
Westphalia. After 1168.

PLATE 13. Monte Cassino Exultet Roll, Christ and Mary Magdalen. Southern Italy. *Circa* 1075.

PLATE 14. Monte Cassino Psalter, Initial 'D'. Southern Italy. First quarter
twelfth century.

QVOD VIDIT ABACVC ppha; VSQ;
quo dñe clamabo & non exaudies.

PLATE 15. Montpellier Bible, Initial 'O': the prophet Habakkuk. Southern France. *Circa* 1125.

ota mea domino reddam in conspectu omnis popli
ti in atriis domus domini in medio tui iherlm.
alis sit quesumus domine uita oratio.
supplicium sicut est in conspectu tuo mors
preciosa scorum ut auriculis peccati libe
rari mereamur futura iherlm prelibari. P.

Alleluia.
audate dnm omnes
gentes: laudate eu
omnes populi
Qm confirmata est sup
nos misedia eius: & ue
ritas domini manet in
eternum. Oro.
mnipotens dominator qui ab omnium
gentium ore laudaris precamur ut di
latet ueritas tua mentem nram et confirmes
sup nos misedia tuam. P.
Alleluia.
onfitemini
domino qm
bonus: qm
in seculum
misedia ei.
Dicat nunc
isrl qm bon.
qm misedi

PLATE 16. La Charité-sur-Loire Psalter, Initial 'L': two monsters, and Initial
'C': the Resurrection. Central France. Late twelfth century.